Classic
Love Poems

SUMMERSDALE

Summersdale Publishers Ltd

46 West Street

Chichester

PO19 1RP

United Kingdom

ISBN 1 873475 55 1

Printed and bound in Great Britain CPD Ltd.

Jacket by Java Jive Design, Chichester.

Contents

Introduction

Of all the stimuli that have inspired poets over the centuries, love in all its guises has been an unceasingly rich and varied source of powerful, romantic and exquisite verse. Love poems have retained their popularity through the years by expressing eternal and universal emotions.

However, not all of the poems in this book celebrate the joys of love: some focus on the anguish of lost or unrequited love, some on jealousy, whilst others would perhaps better be described as poems of 'lust'.

This collection of *Classic Love Poems* has been carefully selected to achieve a balance, a cross section of the true 'classics' of this genre, with a selection of poems from William Blake and Anne Bradstreet to Christina Rossetti and William Shakespeare. The resulting mélange constitutes a thorough representation of the enduring power of love over all mankind.

Inconstancy Reproved

I do confess thou'rt smooth and fair
And I might have gone near to love thee,
Had I not found the slightest prayer
That lips could move, had power to move thee;
But I can let thee now alone
As worthy to be loved by none.

I do confess thou'rt sweet; yet find
Thee such an unthrift of thy sweets,
Thy favours are but like the wind
That kisseth everything it meets:
And since thou canst with more than one,
Thou'rt worthy to be kissed by none.

The morning rose that untouched stands
Armed with her briers, how sweet she smells!
But plucked and strained through ruder hands,
Her sweets no longer with her dwells:
But scent and beauty both are gone,
And leaves fall from her, one by one.

Such fate ere long will thee betide
When thou hast handled been awhile,
With sere flowers to be thrown aside;
And I shall sigh, while some will smile,
To see thy love to every one
Hath brought thee to be loved by none.

Sir Robert Ayton

The Question Answered

What is it men in women do require?
The lineaments of gratified desire.
What is it women do in men require?
The lineaments of gratified desire.

William Blake

I Laid Me Down Upon A Bank

I laid me down upon a bank
Where Love lay sleeping
I heard among the rushes dank
Weeping, Weeping.

Then I went to the heath and the wild
To the thistles and thorns of the waste
And they told me how they were beguil'd
Driven out, and compell'd to be chaste.

William Blake

Love's Secret

Never seek to tell thy love,
Love that never told can be;
For the gentle wind doth move
Silently, invisibly.

I told my love, I told my love,
I told her all my heart,
Trembling, cold, in ghastly fears,
Ah! she did depart!

Soon after she was gone from me,
A traveller came by,
Silently, invisibly:
He took her with a sigh.

William Blake

To My Dear And Loving Husband

If ever two were one, then surely we;
If ever man were loved by wife, then thee;
If ever wife was happy in a man,
Compare with me, ye women, if you can.
I prize thy love more than whole mines of gold,
Or all the riches that the East doth hold.
My love is such that rivers cannot quench,
Nor aught but love from thee give recompense.
Thy love is such I can no way repay;
The heavens reward thee manifold, I pray.
Then while we live in love let's so persevere
That when we live no more we may live ever.

Anne Bradstreet

Life In A Love

Escape me?
Never -
Beloved!
While I am I, and you are you,
So long as the world contains us both,
Me the loving and you the loth,
While the one eludes, must the other pursue.
My life is a fault at last, I fear:
It seems too much like a fate, indeed!
Though I do my best I shall scarce succeed.
But what if I fail of my purpose here?
It is but to keep the nerves at strain,

To dry one's eyes and laugh at a fall
And, baffled, get up to begin again -
So the chase takes up one's life, that's all.
While, look but once from your farthest bound
At me so deep in the dust and dark,
No sooner the old hope drops to ground
Than a new one, straight to the self-same mark

    I shape me -
    Ever
    Removed!

Robert Browning

Never The Time And The Place

Never the time and the place
And the loved one all together!
This path - how soft to pace!
This May - what magic weather!
Where is the loved one's face?
In a dream that loved one's face meets mine,
But the house is narrow, the place is bleak
Where, outside, rain and wind combine
With a furtive ear, if I strive to speak,
With hostile eye at my flushing cheek,
With a malice that marks each word, each sign!
O enemy sly and serpentine
Uncoil thee from the waking man!

Do I hold the past
Thus firm and fast
Yet doubt if the future hold I can

This path so soft to pace shall lead,
Thro' the magic of May to herself indeed!
Or narrow if needs the house must be,
Outside are the storms and strangers: we -
Oh, close, safe, warm sleep I and she,
- I and she!

Robert Browning

A Red, Red Rose

O my Luve's like a red, red rose,
That's newly sprung in June;
O my Luve's like the melodie
That's sweetly play'd in tune.

As fair art thou, my bonnie lass,
So deep in luve am I:
And I will love thee still, my Dear,
Till a' the seas gang dry.

Till a' the seas gang dry, my Dear,
And the rocks melt wi' the sun;
I will love thee still, my Dear,
While the sands o' life shall run.

And fare thee weel, my only Luve,
And fare thee weel, a while!
And I will come again, my Luve,
Tho' it were ten thousand mile!

Robert Burns

I Love My Jean

Of a'the airts the wind can blaw,
I dearly like the west,
For there the bonnie Lassie lives,
The Lassie I lo'e best.
There wild woods grow, and rivers row,
And monie a hill between;
But day and night my fancy's flight
Is ever wi' my Jean.

I see her in the dewy flowers,
I see her sweet and fair;
I hear her in the tunefu' birds
I hear her charm the air:
There's not a bonnie flower that springs
By fountain, shaw, or green;
There's not a bonnie bird that sings
But minds me o' my Jean.

Robert Burns

One Fond Kiss And Then We Sever

One fond kiss, and then we sever!
One farewell, and then forever!
Deep in heart-wrung tears I'll pledge thee
Warring sighs and groans I'll wage thee.

Who shall say that Fortune grieves him,
While the star of Hope she leaves him?
Me, no cheerful twinkle lights me;
Dark despair around benights me.

I'll ne'er blame my partial fancy,
Nothing could resist my Nancy:
But to see her was to love her;
Love but her, and love forever.

Had we never loved so kindly,
Had we never loved so blindly,
Never met or never parted,
We had ne'er been broken-hearted.

Fare thee well, thou first and fairest!
Fare thee well, thou best and dearest!
Thine be every joy and treasure,
Peace, enjoyment, love, and pleasure!

One fond kiss, and then we sever!
One farewell, alas, for ever!
Deep in heart-wrung tears I'll pledge thee,
Warring sighs and groans I'll wage thee.

Robert Burns

She Walks In Beauty

She walks in Beauty, like the night
Of cloudless climes and starry skies;
And all that's best of dark and bright
Meet in her aspect and her eyes:
Thus mellowed to that tender light
Which Heaven to gaudy day denies.

One shade the more, one ray the less,
Had half impaired the nameless grace
Which waves in every raven tress,
Or softly lightens o'er her face;
Where thoughts serenely sweet express
How pure, how dear their dwelling-place.

And on that cheek, and o'er that brow,
So soft, so calm, yet eloquent,
The smiles that win, the tints that glow,
But tell of days in goodness spent,
A mind at peace with all below,
A heart whose love is innocent!

Lord Byron

Stanzas For Music

There be none of Beauty's daughters
With a magic like thee;
And like music on the waters
Is thy sweet voice to me:
When, as if its sound were causing
The charmèd Ocean's pausing,
The waves lie still and gleaming,
And the lull'd winds seem dreaming.

And the Midnight Moon is weaving
Her bright chain o'er the deep;
Whose breast is gently heaving,
As an infant's asleep:
So the spirit bows before thee,
To listen and adore thee;
With a full but soft emotion,
Like the swell of Summer's ocean.

Lord Byron

On Parting

The kiss, dear maid! thy lip has left
Shall never part from mine,
Till happier hours restore the gift
Untainted back to thine.

Thy parting glance, which fondly beams,
An equal love may see:
The tear that from thine eyelid streams
Can weep no change in me.

I ask no pledge to make me blest
In gazing when alone;
Nor one memorial for a breast
Whose thoughts are all thine own.

Nor need I write - to tell the tale
My pen were doubly weak:
Oh! what can idle words avail,
Unless the heart could speak?

By day or night, in weal or woe,
That heart, no longer free,
Must bear the love it cannot show,
And silent ache for thee.

Lord Byron

To Ellen

Oh! might I kiss those eyes of fire,
A million scarce would quench desire:
Still would I steep my lips in bliss,
And dwell an age on every kiss;
Nor then my soul should sated be,
Still would I kiss and cling to thee:
Nought should my kiss from thine dissever;
Still would we kiss, and kiss forever,
E'en though the numbers did exceed
The yellow harvest's countless seed.
To part would be a vain endeavour:
Could I desist? Ah, never-never!

Lord Byron

So We'll Go No More A-Roving

So we'll go no more a-roving
So late into the night,
Though the heart be still as loving,
And the moon be still as bright.

For the sword outwears its sheath,
And the soul wears out the breast,
And the heart must pause to breathe,
And Love itself have rest.

Though the night was made for loving,
And the day returns too soon,
Yet we'll go no more a-roving
By the light of the moon.

Lord Byron

Maid Of Athens

Maid of Athens, ere we part,
Give, oh give me back my heart!
Or, since that has left my breast,
Keep it now, and take the rest
Hear my vow before I go,
Zoë mou, sas agapo.

By those tresses unconfin'd,
Woo'd by each Aegean wind;
By those lids whose jetty fringe
Kiss thy soft cheeks' blooming tinge;
By those wild eyes like the roe,
Zoë mou, sas agapo.

By that lip I long to taste,
By that zone-encircl'd waist,
By all the token-flowers that tell
What words can never speak so well;
By love's alternate joy and woe,
Zoë mou, sas agapo.

Maid of Athens! I am gone:
Think of me, sweet! when alone.
Though I fly to Istambol,
Athens holds my heart and soul:
Can I cease to love thee? No!
Zoë mou, sas agapo.

Lord Byron

Freedom And Love

How delicious is the winning
Of a kiss at Love's beginning,
When two mutual hearts are sighing
For the knot there's no untying!

Yet remember, 'midst our wooing
Love has bliss, but Love has ruing;
Other smiles may make you fickle,
Tears for other charms may trickle.

Love he comes, and Love he tarries,
Just as fate or fancy carries;
Longest stays, when sorest chidden;
Laughs and flies, when press'd and bidden.

Bind the sea to slumber stilly,
Bind its odour to the lily,
Bind the aspen ne'er to quiver,
Then bind Love to last forever.

Love's a fire that needs renewal
Of fresh beauty for its fuel:
Love's wing moults when caged and captured,
Only free, he soars enraptured.

Can you keep the bee from ranging
Or the ringdove's neck from changing?
No! nor fetter'd Love from dying
In the knot there's no untying.

Thomas Campbell

My Lady's Eyes

Mistress, since you so much desire
To know the place of Cupid's fire
In your fair shrine that flame doth rest,
Yet never harboured in your breast.

It bides not in your lips so sweet,
Nor where the rose and lilies meet;
But a little higher, a little higher,
There, there, O there lies Cupid's fire.

Even in those starry piercing eyes,
There Cupid's sacred fire lies;
Those eyes I strive not to enjoy,
For they have power to destroy:

Nor woo for a smile or kiss,
So meanly triumphs not my bliss;
But a little higher, a little higher
I climb to crown my chaste desire.

Thomas Campion

There Is A Garden In Her Face

There is a garden in her face,
Where roses and white lilies grow;
A heavenly paradise is that place,
Wherein all pleasant fruits do grow;
There cherries grow that none may buy
Till 'cherry ripe' themselves do cry.

Those cherries fairly do enclose
Of orient pearl a double row,
Which, when her lovely laughter shows,
They look like rosebuds fill'd with snow;
Yet them no peer nor prince may buy
Till 'cherry ripe' themselves do cry.

Her eyes like angels watch them still,
Her brows like bended bows do stand,
Threatening with piercing frowns to kill
All that approach with eye or hand
These sacred cherries to come nigh,
Till 'cherry' ripe themselves do cry.

Thomas Campion

Come, O Come

Come, O come, my life's delight,
Let me not in languor pine!
Love loves no delay; thy sight,
The more enjoyed, the more divine:
O come, and take from me
The pain of being deprived of thee!

Thou all sweetness dost enclose,
Like a little world of bliss.
Beauty guards thy looks: the rose
In them pure and eternal is.
Come, then, and make thy flight
As swift to me, as heavenly light.

Thomas Campion

Red And White Roses

Read in these Roses the sad story
Of my hard fate, and your owne glory.
In the White you may discover
The paleness of a fainting lover;
In the Red the flames still feeding
On my heart, with fresh wounds bleeding.
The White will tell you how I languish,
And the Red express my anguish;
The White my innocence displaying,
The Red my martyrdom betraying.
The frowns that on your brow resided,
Have those Roses thus divided.
Oh! let your smiles but clear the weather,
And then they both shall grow together.

Thomas Carew

The Compliment

I do not love thee for that fair
Rich fan of thy most curious hair;
Though the wires thereof be drawn
Finer than the threads of lawn,
And are softer than the leaves
On which the subtle spider weaves.

I do not love thee for those flowers
Growing on thy cheeks - love's bowers;
Though such cunning them hath spread,
None can paint them white and red:
Love's golden arrows thence are shot
Yet for them I love thee not.

I do not love thee for those soft
Red coral lips I've kissed so oft;
Nor teeth of pearl, the double guard
To speech whence music still is heard,
Though from those lips a kiss being taken
Might tyrants melt, and death awaken.

I do not love thee, O my fairest,
For that richest, for that rarest
Silver pillar, which stands under
Thy sound head, that globe of wonder;
Though that neck be whiter far
Than towers of polished ivory are.

Thomas Carew

The Unfading Beauty

He that loves a rosy cheek,
Or a coral lip admires,
Or from star-like eyes doth seek
Fuel to maintain his fires:
As old Time makes these decay,
So his flames must waste away.

But a smooth and steadfast mind,
Gentle thoughts and calm desires,
Hearts with equal love combined,
Kindle never-dying fires.
Where these are not, I despise
Lovely cheeks or lips or eyes.

Thomas Carew

To Chloe, Who For His Sake Wished Herself Younger

There are two births; the one when light
First strikes the new awaken'd sense;
The other when two souls unite,
And we must count our life from thence:
When you loved me and I loved you
The both of us were born anew.

Love then to us new souls did give
And in those souls did plant new powers;
Since when another life we live,
The breath we breathe is his, not ours:
Love makes those young whom age doth chill,
And whom he finds young keeps young still.

William Cartwright

No Platonic Love

Tell me no more of minds embracing minds,
And hearts exchang'd for hearts;
That spirits spirits meet, as winds do winds,
And mix their subt'lest parts;
That two unbodied essences may kiss,
And then like angels, twist and feel one bliss.

I was that silly thing that once was wrought
To practise this thin love;
I climb'd from sex to soul, from soul to thought;
But thinking there to move,
Headlong I roll'd from thought to soul, and then
From soul I lighted at the sex agen.

As some strict down-look'd men pretend to fast
Who yet in closets eat;
So lovers who profess they spirits taste,
Feed yet on grosser meat;
I know they boast they souls to souls convey,
Howe'er they meet, the body is the way.

Come, I will undeceive thee, they that tread
Those vain aerial ways,
Are like young heirs and alchymists misled
To waste their wealth and days,
For searching thus to be for ever rich,
They only find a med'cine for the itch.

William Cartwright

The Faithful And The True

Love lives beyond
The tomb, the earth, which fades like dew.
I love the fond,
The faithful, and the true.

Love lives in sleep,
The happiness of healthy dreams:
Eve's dews may weep,
But love delightful seems.

'Tis seen in flowers,
And in the morning's pearly dew;
On earth's green hours
And in the heaven's eternal blue.

'Tis heard in spring
When light and sunbeams, warm and kind,
On angel's wing
Bring love and music to the mind.

And where is voice,
So young, so beautiful, and sweet
As nature's choice,
Where spring and lovers meet.

Love lives beyond
The tomb, the earth, the flowers, and dew.
I love the fond,
The faithful, young, and true.

John Clare

First Love

I ne'er was struck before that hour
With love so sudden and so sweet;
Her face it bloomed like a sweet flower
And stole my heart away complete.
My face turned pale as deadly pale,
My legs refused to walk away,
And when she looked what could I ail?
My life and all seemed turned to clay.

And then my blood rushed to my face
And took my eyesight quite away;
The trees and bushes round the place
Seemed midnight at noonday.

I could not see a single thing,
Words from my eyes did start;
They spoke as chords do from the string
And blood burnt round my heart.

Are flowers the winter's choice?
Is love's bed always snow?
She seemed to hear my silent voice,
Not love's appeals to know.
I never saw so sweet a face
As that I stood before;
My heart has left its dwelling place
And can return no more.

John Clare

Love's Pains

This love, I canna' bear it,
It cheats me night and day;
This love, I canna' wear it
It takes my peace away.

This love, wa' once a flower;
But now it is a thorn -
The joy o' evening hour,
Turn'd to a pain e're morn.

This love, it wa' a bud,
And a secret known to me;
Like a flower within a wood;
Like a nest within a tree.

This love, wrong understood,
Oft' turned my joy to pain;
I tried to throw away the bud,
But the blossom would remain.

John Clare

I Hid My Love

I hid my love when young while I
Could'nt bear the buzzing of a flye;
I hid my love to my despite
Till I could not bear to look at light.
I dare not gaze upon her face
But left her memory in each place,
Where ere I saw a wildflower lye
I kissed and bade my love good bye.

I met her in the greenest dells
Where dewdrops pearl the wood bluebells;
The lost breeze kissed her bright blue eye
The bee kissed and went singing by.

A sunbeam found a passage there,
A gold chain round her neck so fair;
As secret as the wild bee's song,
She lay there all the summer long.

I hid my love in field and town
Till e'en the breeze would knock me down;
The bees seemed singing ballads o'er
The fly's buzz turned a lion's roar.
And even silence found a tongue
To haunt me all the summer long;
The riddle nature could not prove
Was nothing else but secret love.

John Clare

To Mary

I sleep with thee, and wake with thee,
And yet thou art not there;
I fill my arms with thoughts of thee,
And press the common air.
Thy eyes are gazing upon mine,
When thou art out of sight;
My lips are always touching thine,
At morning, noon, and night.

I think and speak of other things
To keep my mind at rest:
But still to thee my memory clings
Like love in woman's breast.

I hide it from the world's wide eye
And think and speak contrary;
But soft the wind comes from the sky,
And whispers tales of Mary.

The night wind whispers in my ear,
The moon shines in my face;
A burden still of chilling fear
I find in every place.
The breeze is whispering in the bush,
And the dews fall from the tree,
All, sighing on, and will not hush
Some pleasant tales of thee.

John Clare

Song

I wish I was where I would be
With love alone to dwell;
Was I but her or she but me
Then love would all be well.
I wish to send my thoughts to her
As quick as thoughts can fly;
But as the winds the waters stir
The mirrors change and flye.

John Clare

The Exchange

We pledged our hearts, my love and I,
I in my arms the maiden clasping;
I could not tell the reason why,
But, O, I trembled like an aspen.

Her father's love she bade me gain;
I went, and shook like any reed!
I strove to act the man - in vain!
We had exchanged our hearts indeed.

Samuel Taylor Coleridge

The Happy Husband

Oft, oft, methinks, the while with thee
I breathe, as from the heart, thy dear
And dedicated name, I hear
A promise and a mystery,
A pledge of more than passing life,
Yea, in that very name of Wife!

A pulse of love that ne'er can sleep!
A feeling that upbraids the heart
With happiness beyond desert,
That gladness half requests to weep!
Nor bless I not the keener sense
And unalarming turbulence.

Of transient joys, that ask no sting
From jealous fears, or coy denying;
But born beneath Love's brooding wing
And into tenderness soon dying,
Wheel out their giddy moment, then
Resign the soul to love again;

A more precipitated vein
Of notes that eddy in the flow
Of smoothest song, they come, they go,
And leave their sweeter understrain
Its own sweet self - a love of Thee
That seems, yet cannot greater be!

Samuel Taylor Coleridge

Song

See, see, she wakes, Sabina wakes!
And now the sun begins to rise;
Less glorious is the morn that breaks
From his bright beams than her fair eyes.

With light united, day they give,
But different fates ere night fulfil.
How many by his warmth will live!
How many will her coldness kill!

William Congreve

The Marriage Ring

The ring, so worn as you behold,
So thin, so pale, is yet of gold:
The passion such it was to prove -
Worn with life's care, love yet was love.

George Crabbe

He Touched Me

He touched me, so I live to know
That such a day, permitted so,
I groped upon his breast.
It was a boundless place to me,
And silenced, as the awful sea
Puts minor streams to rest.

And now, I'm different from before,
As if I breathed superior air,
Or brushed a Royal Gown;
My feet, too, that had wandered so,
My Gypsy Face transfigured now
To tenderer Renown.

Into this Port, if I might come,
Rebecca, to Jerusalem,
Would not so ravished turn -
Nor Persian, baffled at her shrine
Lift such a crucifixal sign
To her imperial sun.

Emily Dickinson

Longing

I envy Seas whereon he rides,
I envy Spokes of Wheels
Of Chariots that him convey,
I envy crooked Hills

That gaze upon his journey;
How easy all can see
What is forbidden utterly
As Heaven, unto me!

I envy Nests of Sparrows
That dot his distant Eaves,
The wealthy Fly upon his Pane,
The happy, happy Leaves

That just abroad his Window
Have Summer's leave to be,
The Ear Rings of Pizarro
Could not obtain for me.

I envy Light that wakes him,
And Bells - that boldly ring
To tell him it is Noon abroad-
Myself be Noon to him,

Yet interdict my Blossom
And abrogate my Bee,
Lest Noon in everlasting Night
Drop Gabriel and me.

Emily Dickinson

Heart, We Will Forget Him

Heart, we will forget him!
You and I, tonight!
You may forget the warmth he gave,
I will forget the light.

When you have done, pray tell me,
That I may straight begin!
Haste! lest while you're lagging,
I may remember him!

Emily Dickinson

Daybreak

Stay, O sweet, and do not rise!
The light that shines comes from their eyes;
The day breaks not: it is my heart,
Because that you and I must part.
Stay! or else my joys will die
And perish in their infancy.

John Donne

A Lecture Upon The Shadow

Stand still, and I will read to thee
A Lecture, Love, in love's philosophy.
These three hours that we have spent,
Walking here, Two shadowes went
Along with us, which we ourselves produced;
But, now the Sunne is just above our head,
We do those shadowes tread;
And to brave clearnesse all things are reduced.
So whilst our infant loves did grow,
Disguises did, and shadows, flow,
From us, and our care; but, now 'tis not so.

That love hath not attained the high'st degree
Which is still diligent lest others see.

Except our loves at this noone stay,
We shall new shadows make the other way.
As the first were made to blinde
Others; these which come behinde
Will work upon ourselves, and blind our eyes.
If our loves faint, and westwardly decline;
To me thou, falsely, thine,
And I to thee mine actions shall disguise.
The morning shadowes wear away,
But these grow longer all the day,
But oh, love's day is short, if love decay.

Love is a growing, or full constant light;
And his first minute, after noon, is night.

John Donne

Ah, How Sweet

Ah, how sweet it is to love,
Ah, how gay is young desire!
And what pleasing pains we prove
When we first approach Love's fire!
Pains of Love are sweeter far
Than all other pleasures are.

Sighs which are from Lovers blown
Do but gently heave the Heart:
Ev'n the tears they shed alone
Cure, like trickling Balm, their smart.
Lovers, when they lose their breath,
Bleed away in easie death.

Love and Time with reverence use,
Treat 'em like a parting friend:
Nor the golden gifts refuse
Which in youth sincere they send:
For each year their price is more,
And they less simple than before.

Love, like Spring-tides full and high,
Swells in every youthful vein:
But each Tide does less supply,
Till they quite shrink in again.
If a flow in Age appear,
'Tis but rain, and runs not clear.

John Dryden

To A Lady
How Long He Would Love Her

It is not, Celia, in our power
To say how long our love will last;
It may be we within this hour
May lose those joys we now do taste:
The blessed, that immortal be,
From change in love are only free.

Then since we mortal lovers are,
Ask not how long our love will last;
But while it does, let us take care
Each minute be with pleasure passed:
Were it not madness to deny
To live because we're sure to die?

George Etherege

I Love My Love In The Morning

I love my love in the morning,
For she like morn is fair -
Her blushing cheek, its crimson streak,
It clouds her golden hair.
Her glance, its beam, so soft and kind;
Her tears, its dewy showers;
And her voice, the tender whispering wind
That stirs the early bowers.

I love my love in the morning,
I love my love at noon,
For she is bright as the lord of light,
Yet mild as autumn's moon:

Her beauty is my bosom's sun
Her faith my fostering shade,
And I will love my darling one,
Till even the sun shall fade.

I love my love in the morning,
I love my love at even;
Her smile's soft play is like the ray
That lights the western heaven:
I loved her when the sun was high,
I loved her when he rose;
But best of all when evening's sigh
Was murmuring at its close.

Gerald Griffin

To The Virgins, To Make Much Of Time

Gather ye Rose-buds while ye may,
Old Time is still a-flying:
And this same flower that smiles today
Tomorrow will be dying.

The glorious Lamp of Heaven, the Sun,
The higher he's a-getting,
The sooner will his Race be run
And nearer he's to Setting.

That Age is best which is the first,
When Youth and Blood are warmer;
But being spent, the worse, and worst
Times still succeed the former.

Then be not coy, but use your time,
And while ye may, go marry:
For having lost but once your prime,
You may for ever tarry.

Robert Herrick

To Anthea, Who May Command Him Anything

Bid me to live, and I will live
Thy Protestant to be;
Or bid me love, and I will give
A loving heart to thee.

A heart as soft, a heart as kind,
A heart as sound and free,
As in the whole world thou canst find,
That heart I'll give to thee.

Bid that heart stay, and it will stay
To honour thy Decree;
Or bid it languish quite away,
And't shall do so for thee.

Bid me to weep, and I will weep,
While I have eyes to see;
And having none, yet I will keep
A heart to weep for thee.

Bid me despaire, and I'll despaire
Under that Cypresse tree:
Or bid me die, and I will dare
E'en Death to die for thee.

Thou art my life, my love, my heart,
The very eyes of me;
And hast command of every part,
To live and die for thee.

Robert Herrick

To Electra

I dare not ask a kiss,
I dare not beg a smile,
Lest having that, or this,
I might grow proud the while.

No, no, the utmost share
Of my desire shall be,
Only to kiss that air,
That lately kissèd thee.

Robert Herrick

The Rock Of Rubies: And The Quarrie Of Pearls

Some ask'd me where the Rubies grew?
And nothing did I say,
But with my finger pointed to
The lips of Julia.

Some ask'd how Pearls did grow, and where?
Then spoke I to my Girle,
To part her lips and shew'd them there
The Quarelets of Pearl.

One asked me where the roses grew;
I bade him not go seek,
But forthwith bade my Julia show
A bud in either cheek.

Robert Herrick

I Love Thee

I love thee - I love thee!
'Tis all that I can say;
It is my vision in the night,
My dreaming in the day;
The very echo of my heart,
The blessing when I pray.
I love thee - I love thee!

I love thee - I love thee!
Is ever on my tongue.
In all my proudest poesy
That chorus still is sung;
It is the verdict of my eyes
Amidst the gay and young:
I love thee - I love thee!
A thousand maids among.

I love thee - I love thee!
Thy bright and hazel glance,
The mellow lute upon those lips,
Whose tender tones entrance.
But most dear heart of hearts, thy proofs.
That still these words enhance!
I love thee - I love thee!
Whatever be thy chance.

Thomas Hood

The Time Of Roses

It was not in the Winter
Our loving lot was cast;
It was the Time of Roses -
We pluck'd them as we pass'd!

'Twas twilight, and I bade you go,
But still you held me fast;
It was the Time of Roses -
We pluck'd them as we pass'd!

What else could peer thy glowing cheek,
That tears began to stud?
And when I ask'd the like of Love
You snatch'd a damask bud,

And oped it to the dainty core,
Still glowing to the last;
It was the Time of Roses -
We pluck'd them as we pass'd!

Thomas Hood

Ruth

She stood breast-high amid the corn,
Clasped by the golden light of morn,
Like the sweetheart of the sun,
Who many a glowing kiss had won.

On her cheek an autumn flush,
Deeply ripened; such a blush
In the midst of brown was born,
Like red poppies grown with corn.

Round her eyes her tresses fell,
Which were blackest none could tell,
But long lashes veiled a light,
That had else been all too bright.

And her hat, with shady brim,
Made her tressy forehead dim ·
Thus she stood amid the stooks,
Praising God with sweetest looks:

Sure, I said, heaven did not mean,
Where I reap thou shouldst but glean,
Lay thy sheaf adown and come,
Share my harvest and my home.

Thomas Hood

Only We

Dream no more that grief and pain
Could such hearts as ours enchain,
Safe from loss and safe from gain,
    Free, as love makes free.

When false friends pass coldly by,
Sigh, in earnest pity, sigh,
Turning thine unclouded eye
    Up from them to me.

Hear not danger's trampling feet,
Feel not sorrow's wintry sleet
Trust that life is just and meet,
    With mine arm round thee.

Lip on lip, and eye to eye,
Love to love, we live, we die;
No more thou, and no more I,
    We, and only we!

Richard Monckton Milnes, Lord Houghton

To Celia

Drink to me only with thine eyes,
And I will pledge with mine;
Or leave a kiss but in the cup
And I'll not look for wine.
The thirst that from the soul doth rise
Doth ask a drink divine;
But might I of Jove's nectar sup
I would not change for thine.

I sent thee late a rosy wreath,
Not so much honouring thee
As giving it a hope, that there
It could not wither'd be;
But thou thereon did'st only breathe
And sent'st it back to me;
Since when it grows, and smells, I swear,
Not of itself, but thee.

Ben Jonson

A Vision Of Beauty

It was a beauty that I saw -
So pure, so perfect, as the frame
Of all the universe were lame
To that one figure, could I draw,
Or give least line of it a law:
A skein of silk without a knot !
A fair march made without a halt!
A curious form without a fault !
A printed book without a blot!
All beauty! - and without a spot.

Ben Jonson

Those Eyes

Ah! do not wanton with those eyes,
Lest I be sick with seeing -
Nor cast them down, but let them rise,
Lest shame destroy their being.

Ah! be not angry with those fires,
For then their threats will kill me;
Nor look too kind on my desires,
For then my hopes will spill me.

Ah! do not steep them in thy tears,
For so will sorrow slay me;
Nor spread them as distraught with fears -
Mine own enough betray me.

Ben Jonson

To Fanny

I cry your mercy - pity - love! - ay, love! -
Merciful love that tantalizes not,
One-thoughted, never-wandering, guileless love,
Unmask'd, and being seen - without a blot!
O! let me have thee whole - all - all - be mine!
That shape, that fairness, that sweet minor zest
Of love, your kiss - those hands, those eyes divine,
That warm, white, lucent, million-pleasured breast -
Yourself - your soul - in pity give me all,
Withhold no atom's atom or I die,
Or living on perhaps, your wretched thrall,
Forget, in the midst of idle misery,
Life's purposes - the palate of my mind
Losing its gust, and my ambition blind!

John Keats

Sonnet

Bright star, would I was steadfast as thou art -
Not in lone splendour hung aloft the night,
And watching, with eternal lids apart,
Like Nature's patient sleepless Eremite,
The moving waters at their priest-like task
Of pure ablution round earth's human shores,
Or gazing on the new soft-fallen mask
Of snow upon the mountains and the moors -
No - yet still steadfast, still unchangeable,
Pillow'd upon my fair love's ripening breast,
To feel for ever its soft fall and swell,
Awake for ever in a sweet unrest,
Still, still to hear her tender-taken breath,
And so live ever - or else swoon to death.

John Keats

Love's Pursuit

Turn I my looks unto the skies,
Love with his arrows wounds mine eyes:
If so I gaze upon the ground,
Love then in every flower is found:
Search I the shade to fly my pain,
He meets me in the shade again:
Wend I to walk in secret grove,
Ev'n there I melt with sacred Love:
If so I bain me in the spring,
Ev'n on the brink I hear him sing:
If so I meditate alone,
He will be partner of my moan:
If so I mourn, he weeps with me,
And where I am, there will he be.
When as I talk of Rosalind,

The god from coyness waxeth kind,
And seems in selfsame flames to fry,
Because he loves as well as I;
Sweet Rosalind, for pity, rue!
For why, than love I am more true:
He, if he speed, will quickly fly;
But in thy love I live and die.

Thomas Lodge

The Passionate Shepherd To His Love

Come live with me and be my love,
And we will all the pleasures prove
That valleys, groves, hills and fields,
Or woods or steepy mountain yields.

And we will sit upon the rocks,
And see the shepherds feed their flocks
By shallow rivers, to whose falls
Melodious birds sing madrigals.

And I will make thee beds of roses
And a thousand fragrant posies;
A cap of flowers, and a kirtle
Embroidered all with leaves of myrtle.

A gown made of the finest wool
Which from our pretty lambs we pull;
Fair linèd slippers for the cold,
With buckles of the purest gold.

A belt of straw and ivy-buds
With coral clasps and amber studs:
And if these pleasures may thee move,
Come live with me and be my love.

Thy shepherd swains shall dance and sing
For thy delight each May morning:
If these delights thy mind may move,
Then live with me and be my love.

Christopher Marlowe

The Definition of Love

My Love is of a birth as rare
As 'tis, for object, strange and high;
It was begotten by Despair
Upon Impossibility.

Magnanimous Despair alone
Could show me so divine a thing,
Where feeble hope could ne'er have flown
But vainly flapped its tinsel wing.

And yet I quickly might arrive
Where my extended soul is fixed;
But Fate does iron wedges drive,
And always crowds itself betwixt.

For Fate with jealous eye does see
Two perfect loves, nor lets them close;
Their union would her ruin be,
And her tyrannic power depose.

And therefore her decrees of steel
Us as the distant poles have placed
(Though Love's whole world on us doth
wheel),
Not by themselves to be embraced,

Unless the giddy heaven fall,
And earth some new convulsion tear,
And, us to join, the world should all
Be cramped into the planisphere.

As lines, so loves oblique may well
Themselves in every angle greet;
But ours, so truly parallel,
Though infinite can never meet.

Therefore the love which us doth bind,
But Fate so enviously debars,
Is the conjunction of the mind,
And opposition of the stars.

Andrew Marvell

When I Would Image

When I would image her features,
Comes up a shrouded head:
I touch the outlines, shrinking;
She seems of the wandering dead.

But when love asks for nothing,
And lies on his bed of snow,
The face slips under my eyelids,
All in its living glow.

Like a dark cathedral city,
Whose spires, and domes, and towers
Quiver in violet lightnings,
My soul basks on for hours.

George Meredith

The Monopolist

If I were yonder wave, my dear,
And thou the isle it clasps around,
I would not let a foot come near
My land of bliss, my fairy ground!

If I were yonder conch of gold,
And thou the pearl within it placed,
I would not let an eye behold
The sacred gem my arms embraced!

If I were yonder orange tree,
And thou the blossom blooming there,
I would not yield a breath of thee,
To scent the most imploring air!

Thomas Moore

Oh, No - Not Ev'n When We First Lov'd

Oh, no - not ev'n when first we lov'd
Wert thou as dear as now thou art;
Thy beauty then my senses mov'd
But now thy virtues bind my heart.
What was but Passion's sigh before
Has since been turn'd to Reason's vow;
And, though I then might love thee more,
Trust me, I love thee better now.

Although my heart in earlier youth
Might kindle with more wild desire,
Believe me, it has gain'd in truth
Much more than it has lost in fire.
The flame now warms my inmost core
That then but sparkled o'er my brow
And though I seem'd to love thee more
Yet, oh, I love thee better now.

Thomas Moore

When I Loved You

When I loved you, I can't but allow
I had many an exquisite minute;
But the scorn that I feel for you now
Hath even more luxury in it!

Thus, whether we're on or we're off
Some witchery seems to await you;
To love you is pleasant enough,
But oh! 'tis delicious to hate you!

Thomas Moore

Across The Sky

Across the sky the daylight crept,
And birds grew garrulous in the grove,
And on my marriage-morn I slept
A soft sleep undisturb'd by love.

Coventry Patmore

A Farewell

With all my will, but much against my heart,
We two now part.
My very dear,
Our solace is, the sad road lies so clear.
It needs no art,
With faint, averted feet
And many a tear,
In our opposed paths to persevere.
Go thou to east, I west.
We will not say
There's any hope, it is so far away.
But, O, my best,
When the one darling of our widowhead,
The nursling Grief,
Is dead,
And no dews blur our eyes

To see the peach-bloom come in evening skies,
Perchance we may,
Where now this night is day,
And even through faith of still averted feet,
Making full circle of our banishment,
Amazed meet;
The bitter journey to the bourne so sweet
Seasoning the termless feast of our content
With tears of recognition never dry.

Coventry Patmore

To Helen

Helen, thy beauty is to me
Like those Nicèan barks of yore
That gently, o'er a perfumed sea,
The weary way-worn wanderer bore
To his own native shore.

On desperate seas long wont to roam,
Thy hyacinth hair, thy classic face,
Thy Naiad airs have brought me home
To the glory that was Greece,
And the grandeur that was Rome.

Lo, in yon brilliant window-niche
How statue-like I see thee stand,
The agate lamp within thy hand,
Ah! Psyche, from the regions which
Are holy land!

Edgar Allan Poe

To One In Paradise

Thou wast all that to me, love,
For which my soul did pine:
A green isle in the sea, love,
A fountain and a shrine
All wreathed with fairy fruits and flowers,
And all the flowers were mine.

Ah, dream too bright to last:
Ah, starry Hope, that didst arise
But to be overcast!
A voice from out the Future cries,
"On! on!" - but o'er the Past
(Dim gulf) my spirit hovering lies
Mute, motionless, aghast.

For, alas! alas! with me
The light of Life is o'er!
No more - no more - no more -
(Such language holds the solemn sea
To the sands upon the shore!)
Shall bloom the thunder-blasted tree,
Or the stricken eagle soar.

And all my days are trances,
And all my nightly dreams
Are where thy dark eye glances,
And where thy footstep gleams -
In what ethereal dances,
By what eternal streams.

Edgar Allan Poe

The Nymph's Reply To The Shepherd

If all the world and love were young,
And truth in every shepherd's tongue,
These pretty pleasures might me move
To live with thee and be thy love.

But Time drives flocks from field to fold;
When rivers rage and rocks grow cold;
And Philomel becometh dumb;
The rest complains of cares to come.

The flowers do fade, and wanton fields
To wayward Winter reckoning yields:
A honey tongue, a heart of gall,
Is fancy's spring, but sorrow's fall.

Thy gowns, thy shoes, thy beds of roses,
Thy cap, thy kirtle, and thy posies,
Soon break, soon wither, soon forgotten -
In folly ripe, in reason rotten.

Thy belt of straw and ivy - buds,
Thy coral clasps and amber studs -
All these in me no means can move
To come to thee and be thy love.

But could youth last, and love still breed,
Had joys no date, nor age no need,
Then these delights my mind might move
To live with thee and be thy love.

Sir Walter Raleigh

A Devout Lover

I have a mistress, for perfections rare
In every eye, but in my thoughts most fair.
Like tapers on the altar shine her eyes;
Her breath is the perfume of sacrifice;
And wheresoe'er my fancy would begin,
Still her perfection lets religion in.
We sit and talk, and kiss away the hours
As chastely as the morning dews kiss flowers:
I touch her, like my beads, with devout care,
And come unto my courtship as my prayer.

Thomas Randolph

Remember

Remember me when I am gone away,
Gone far away into the silent land;
When you can no more hold me by the hand,
Nor I half turn to go, yet turning stay.
Remember me when no more day by day
You tell me of our future that you planned;
Only remember me; you understand
It will be late to counsel then or pray.
Yet if you should forget me for a while
And afterwards remember, do not grieve:
For if the darkness and corruption leave
A vestige of the thoughts that once I had,
Better by far you should forget and smile
Than you should remember and be sad.

Christina Rossetti

Grown And Flown

I loved my love from green of Spring
Until sere Autumn's fall;
But now that leaves are withering
How should one love at all?
One heart's too small
For hunger, cold, love, everything.

I loved my love on sunny days
Until late Summer's wane;
But now that frost begins to glaze
How should one love again?
Nay, love and pain
Walk wide apart in diverse ways.

I loved my love - alas to see
That this should be, alas!
I thought that this could scarcely be,
Yet has it come to pass:
Sweet sweet love was,
Now bitter bitter grown to me.

Christina Rossetti

Sudden Light

I have been here before,
But when or how I cannot tell:
I know the grass beyond the door,
The sweet keen smell,
The sighing sound, the lights around the
shore.

You have been mine before -
How long ago I may not know:
But just when at that swallow's soar
Your neck turned so,
Some veil did fall, - I knew it all of yore.

Has this been thus before?
And shall not thus time's eddying flight
Still with our lives our love restore
In death's despite
And day and night yield one delight once
more?

Dante Gabriel Rossetti

Love As The Theme Of Poets

And said I that my limbs were old;
And said I that my blood was cold,
And that my kindly fire was fled,
And my poor withered heart was dead,
And that I might not sing of love?
How could I to the dearest theme,
That ever warmed a minstrel's dream
So foul, so false, a recreant prove!
How could I name love's very name
Nor wake my harp to notes of flame!

In peace, Love tunes the shepherd's reed;
In war, he mounts the warrior's steed;
In halls, in gay attire is seen;
In hamlets, dances on the green.
Love rules the court, the camp, the grove,
And men below, and saints above;
For love is heaven, and heaven is love.

Sir Walter Scott

To Cloris

Cloris, I cannot say your eyes
Did my unwary heart surprise;
Nor will I swear it was your face,
Your shape, or any nameless grace:
For you are so entirely fair,
To love a part, injustice were;
No drowning man can know which drop
Of water his last breath did stop;
So when the stars in heaven appear,
And join to make the night look clear;
The light we no one's bounty call,
But the obliging gift of all.
He that does lips or hands adore,
Deserves them only, and no more;

But I love all, and every part,
And nothing less can ease my heart.
Cupid, that lover, weakly strikes,
Who can express what 'tis he likes.

Sir Charles Sedley

Sonnet

Shall I compare thee to a Summer's day?
Thou art more lovely and more temperate:
Rough winds do shake the darling buds of May.
And Summer's lease hath all too short a date:
Sometimes too hot the eye of heaven shines,
And often is it's gold complexion dimm'd;
And every fair from fair sometimes declines,
By chance or nature's changing course untrimm'd:
But thy eternal Summer shall not fade
Nor lose possession of that fair thou owest;
Nor shall Death brag thou wanderest in the shade,
When in eternal lines to time thou growest:
So long as men can breathe, or eyes can see,
So long lives this, and this gives life to thee.

William Shakespeare

Take, O take those Lips away

Take, O take those lips away,
That so sweetly were forsworn;
And those eyes, the break of day,
Lights that do mislead the morn!
But my kisses bring again,
            Bring again;
Seals of love, but seal'd in vain,
            Seal'd in vain!

William Shakespeare

Sonnet

Let me not to the marriage of true minds
Admit impediments. Love is not love
Which alters when it alteration finds,
Or bends with the remover to remove:
O, no; it is ever-fixed mark,
That looks on tempests and is never shaken;
It is the star to every wandering bark,
Whose worth's unknown, although his height be taken.
Love's not Time's fool, though rosy lips and cheeks
Within his bending sickle's compass come;
Love alters not with his brief hours and weeks,
But bears it out even to the edge of doom.
If this be error and upon me prov'd,
I never writ, nor no man ever lov'd.

William Shakespeare

Sonnet

My love is strengthen'd though more weak in seeming;
I love not less, though less the show appear;
That love is merchandised whose rich esteeming
The owner's tongue doth publish everywhere.
Our love was new, and then but in the spring,
When I was wont to greet it with my lays;
As Philomel in summer's front doth sing
And stops her pipe in growth of riper days:
Not that the summer is less pleasant now
Than when her mournful hymns did hush the night,
But that wild music burthens every bough,
And sweets grown common lose their dear delight.
Therefore, like her, I sometime hold my tongue,
Because I would not dull you with my song.

William Shakespeare

Love's Philosophy

The fountains mingle with the river
And the rivers with the Ocean,
The winds of Heaven mix for ever
With a sweet emotion;
Nothing in the world is single;
All things by a law divine
In one spirit meet and mingle.
Why not I with thine? ·

See the mountains kiss high Heaven
And the waves clasp one another;
No sister-flower would be forgiven
If it disdained its brother;
And the sunlight clasps the earth
And the moonbeams kiss the sea:
What is all this sweet work worth
If thou kiss not me?

Percy Bysshe Shelley

I Arise From Dreams Of Thee

I arise from dreams of thee
In the first sweet sleep of night,
When the winds are breathing low,
And the stars are shining bright.
I arise from dreams of thee,
And a spirit in my feet
Hath led me - who knows how? -
To thy chamber window, Sweet!

The wandering airs they faint
On the dark, the silent stream -
The Champak odours fail
Like sweet thoughts in a dream;
The nightingale's complaint,

It dies upon her heart,
As I must die on thine,
O, beloved as thou art!

O, lift me from the grass!
I die, I faint!, I fail!
Let thy love in kisses rain
On my lips and eyelids pale.
My cheek is cold and white, alas!
My heart beats loud and fast:
Oh! press it close to thine again,
Where it will break at last.

Percy Bysshe Shelley

When Passion's Trance Is Overpast

When passion's trance is overpast,
If tenderness and truth could last,
Or live, whilst all wild feelings keep
Some mortal slumber, dark and deep,
I should not weep, I should not weep!

It were enough to feel, to see,
Thy soft eyes gazing tenderly,
And dream the rest - and burn and be
The secret food of fires unseen,
Couldst thou but be as thou hast been.

After the slumber of the year
The woodland violets reappear;
All things revive in field or grove,
And sky and sea, but two, which move
And form all others - life, and love.

Percy Byshhe Shelley

To ·

One word is too often profaned
For me to profane it,
One feeling too falsely disdained
For thee to disdain it;
One hope is too like despair
For prudence to smother,
And pity from thee more dear
Than that from another.

I can give not what men call love,
But wilt thou accept not
The worship the heart lifts above
And the Heavens reject not -
The desire of the moth for the star,
Of the night for the morrow,
The devotion to something afar
From the sphere of our sorrow?

Percy Bysshe Shelley

The Stolen Heart

I prythee send me back my heart
Since I cannot have thine;
For if from yours you will not part,
Why then shouldst thou have mine?

Yet now I think on't, let it lie;
To find it were in vain,
For thou'st a thief in either eye
Would steal it back again.

Why should two hearts in one breast lie,
And yet not lodge together?
O love! where is thy sympathy,
If thus our breasts you sever?

But love is such a mystery,
I cannot find it out;
For when I think I'm best resolved
I then am most in doubt.

Then farewell love, and farewell woe,
I will no longer pine;
For I'll believe I have her heart
As much as she hath mine.

Sir John Suckling

On Stella's Birthday

Stella this day is thirty-four
(We shan't dispute a year or more),
However Stella, be not troubled,
Although thy size and years are doubled,
Since first I saw thee at sixteen
The brightest virgin on the green,
So little is thy form declin'd
Made up so largely in thy mind.
Oh, would it please the Gods to split
Thy beauty, size, and years, and wit,
No age could furnish out a pair
Of nymphs so graceful, wise and fair
With half the lustre of your eyes,
With half your wit, your years and size:

And then before it grew too late,
How should I beg of gentle fate
(That either nymph might have her swain)
To split my worship too in twain.

Jonathan Swift

Oblation

Ask nothing more of me, sweet;
All I can give you I give;
Heart of my heart, were it more,
More should be laid at your feet:
Love that should help you to live -
Song that should spur you to soar.

All things were nothing to give,
Once to have sense of you more -
Touch you and taste of you, sweet,
Think you and breathe you, and live
Swept of your wings as they soar,
Trodden by chance of your feet.

I, who have love and no more,
Bring you but love of you, sweet.
He that hath more, let him give;
He that hath wings, let him soar:
Mine is the heart at your feet
Here, that must love you to live.

Algernon Charles Swinburne

Like The Touch of Rain

Like the touch of rain she was
On a man's flesh and hair and eyes
When the joy of walking thus
Has taken him by surprise:

With the love of the storm he burns,
He sings, he laughs, well I know how,
But forgets when he returns
As I shall not forget her 'Go now.'

Those two shut a door
Between me and the blessed rain
That was never shut before
And will not open again.

Edward Thomas

Yes! Thou Art Fair

Yes! thou art fair, yet be not moved
To scorn the declaration,
That sometimes I in thee have loved
My fancy's own creation.

Imagination needs must stir:
Dear maid, this truth believe,
Minds that have nothing to confer
Find little to perceive.

Be pleased that nature made thee fit
To feed my heart's devotion,
By laws to which all forms submit
In sky, air, earth, and ocean.

William Wordsworth

What Heavenly Smiles!

What heavenly smiles! O Lady mine
Through my very heart they shine;
And, if my brow gives back their light,
Do thou look gladly on the sight;
As the clear Moon with modest pride
Beholds her own bright beams,
Reflected from the mountain's side
And from the headlong streams.

William Wordsworth

To ·

Let other bards of angels sing,
Bright suns without a spot;
But thou art no such perfect thing:
Rejoice that thou art not!

Heed not tho' none should call thee fair:
So, Mary, let it be
If naught in loveliness compare
With what thou art to me.

True beauty dwells in deep retreats,
Whose veil is unremoved
Till heart with heart in concord beats,
And the lover is beloved.

William Wordsworth

Behold, Love, Thy Power

Behold, love, thy power how she despiseth!
My great pain how little she regardeth!
The holy oath, whereof she taketh no cure,
Broken she hath; and yet she bideth sure
Right at her ease and little she dreadeth.
Weaponed thou art, and she unarmed sitteth;
To the disdainful her life she leadeth,
To me spiteful without cause or measure,
      Behold, love.

I am in hold: if pity thee moveth,
Go bend thy bow, that stony hearts breaketh,
And with some stroke revenge the displeasure
Of thee and him, that sorrow doth endure,
And, as his lord, the lowly entreateth.
　　Behold, love.

Sir Thomas Wyatt

A Drinking Song

Wine comes in at the mouth
And love comes in at the eye;
That's all we know for truth
Before we grow old and die.
I lift the glass to my mouth,
I look at you, and I sigh.

W.B. Yeats

After Long Silence

Speech after long silence; it is right,
All other lovers being estranged or dead,
Unfriendly lamplight hid under its shade,
The curtains drawn upon unfriendly night,
That we descant and yet again descant
Upon the supreme theme of Art and Song:
Bodily decrepitude is wisdom; young
We loved each other and were ignorant.

W. B. Yeats

To An Isle In The Water

Shy one, shy one,
Shy one of my heart.
She moves in the firelight
Pensively apart.

She carries in the dishes,
And lays them in a row.
To an isle in the water
With her would I go.

She carries in the candles,
And lights the curtained room.
Shy in the doorway
And shy in the gloom;

And shy as a rabbit,
Helpful and shy.
To an isle in the water
With her would I fly.

W. B. Yeats

Brown Penny

I whispered, 'I am too young,'
And then, 'I am old enough';
Wherefore I threw a penny
To find out if I might love,
'Go and love, go and love, young man,
If the lady be young and fair.'
Ah, penny, brown penny, brown penny,
I am looped in the loops of her hair.

O love is the crooked thing
There is nobody wise enough
To find out all that is in it,
For he would be thinking of love
Till the stars had run away
And the shadows eaten the moon.
Ah, penny, brown penny, brown penny,
One cannot begin it too soon.

W. B. Yeats

When You Are Old

When you are old and grey and full of sleep,
And nodding by the fire, take down this book,
And slowly read, and dream of the soft look
Your eyes had once, and of their shadows deep;

How many loved your moments of glad grace,
And loved your beauty with love false or true;
But one man loved the pilgrim soul in you,
And loved the sorrows of your changing face.

And bending down beside the glowing bars
Murmur, a little sadly, how Love fled
And paced upon the mountains overhead
And hid his face amid a crowd of stars.

W. B. Yeats